HOW DO Spiders HEAR?

by Nancy Furstinger

Content Consultant

Michael L. Draney, PhD
Department of Natural and Applied Sciences
University of Wisconsin-Green Bay

CAPSTONE PRESS
a capstone imprint

Bright Idea Books are published by Capstone Press
1710 Roe Crest Drive, North Mankato, Minnesota 56003
www.mycapstone.com

Library of Congress Cataloging-in-Publication Data
Names: Furstinger, Nancy, author.
Title: How do spiders hear? / by Nancy Furstinger.
Description: North Mankato, Minnesota : Capstone Press, 2019. | Series: Crazy animal facts |
    Includes bibliographical references and index.
Identifiers: LCCN 2018018700 (print) | LCCN 2018021634 (ebook) | ISBN 9781543541564 (ebook) |
    ISBN 9781543541168 (hardcover : alk. paper)
Subjects: LCSH: Spiders--Juvenile literature.
Classification: LCC QL452.2 (ebook) | LCC QL452.2 .F86 2019 (print) | DDC 595.4/4--dc23
LC record available at https://lccn.loc.gov/2018018700

Editorial Credits
Editor: Maddie Spalding
Designer: Becky Daum
Production Specialist: Colleen McLaren

Photo Credits
iStockphoto: jerbarber, 6–7, Joe_Guetzloff, 24–25, KirsanovV, 25; Newscom: H. Bellmann/
picture alliance/blickwinkel/H, 19, Mark Moffett/Minden Pictures, 26–27; Shutterstock
Images: Aleks Melnik, cover (music notes), Alen thien, 9, 28, Cathy Keifer, 5, 20–21, 30–31,
davemhuntphotography, 10–11, dmvphotos, 23, Dr Morley Read, 14–15, 16–17, Krom1975, cover
(spider), MF Photo, 12–13

Design Elements: iStockphoto, Red Line Editorial, and Shutterstock Images

TABLE OF CONTENTS

CHAPTER 1

TRAPPED!

A spider waits. It sits at the edge of its web. A fly buzzes nearby. It doesn't see the web. It zooms into the trap. The web is made of silk. The silk is sticky. The fly can't escape.

Spiders use webs to catch flies and other insects.

A spider rolls its prey in silk to make sure it cannot escape.

The spider doesn't have ears. It has eyes. But its eyes cannot see well. Still, the spider can sense the fly's movement. The spider moves quickly to its **prey**. It sinks its **fangs** into the fly. The fangs deliver **venom**. The fly cannot move. The spider wraps the fly in silk. It will save this meal for later.

CHAPTER 2

HEARING
with Hairs

Scientists once thought spiders were deaf. Then scientists discovered something amazing. Spiders don't need ears. They have other ways of sensing sounds.

Scientists have studied spiders, such as the jumping spider, to discover how they sense sounds.

HAIR EVERYWHERE

Spiders are super hairy.

Their bodies are covered in hairs.

Some of their leg hairs have

a special purpose. They help

spiders sense sounds.

Some spiders, such as tarantulas, are hairier than others.

Sound travels when air moves back and forth. These movements are **sound waves**. Humans have ears. Inside each ear is an eardrum. The eardrum is a **membrane**. Sound reaches the eardrum. The eardrum **vibrates**. Other parts of the ear vibrate too. This includes tiny bones in the ear. The movement carries a message to the brain. The brain identifies the sound.

Spiders sense sounds differently. Sound waves wiggle special hairs on a spider's legs. The spider feels the movement.

Special leg hairs
help a spider sense
movement.

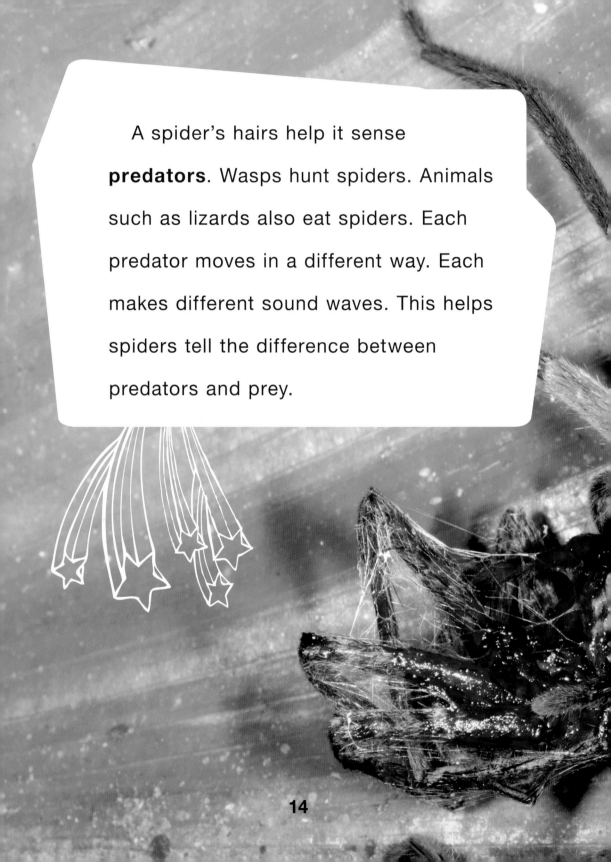

A spider's hairs help it sense **predators**. Wasps hunt spiders. Animals such as lizards also eat spiders. Each predator moves in a different way. Each makes different sound waves. This helps spiders tell the difference between predators and prey.

Some spiders eat other spiders.

SPECIAL ORGANS

Spiders have **organs** on their legs. A spider has an outer shell. This is a skeleton on the outside of the spider's body. It is called an **exoskeleton**. The organs are on this shell. They are made up of tiny slits. Each slit is a different length. The slits look like harp strings. Vibrations cause the slits to change shape. This helps the spider sense movement.

slits

slit organ

A spider's leg organs are made up of many tiny slits.

EXOSKELETONS

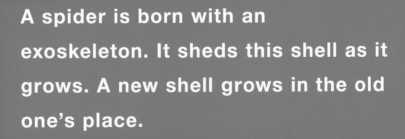

A spider is born with an exoskeleton. It sheds this shell as it grows. A new shell grows in the old one's place.

CHAPTER 3

FINDING a Mate

The slits on a spider's legs help it find a **mate**. Some male spiders scratch leaves. They do this with their mouths. Some also drum on leaves.

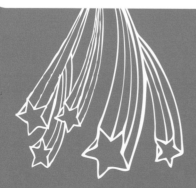

18

They use their **abdomens** to do this.

Female spiders feel the movements.

The slits on their legs change shape.

This lets them know a mate is on

the plant.

Some spiders find mating partners by scratching on leaves.

PURRING SPIDERS

Some male wolf spiders purr to find mates. The spider finds a dead leaf. It taps the leaf with its body. This makes the leaf vibrate. The leaf acts like a phone line. Sound waves travel through it.

WOLF SPIDERS

A wolf spider's purrs are so loud that humans can hear them.

Dead and dry leaves carry sound farther than leaves that are not dry.

The waves hit leaves near a female spider. The slits on the female's legs change shape. The female knows a mate is near.

CHAPTER 4

MUSICAL
Spiders

A spider makes silk in its body. It pushes out silk through an organ. The organ is in its abdomen. Silk is strong. It is also flexible. It can stretch without breaking. Prey gets caught in the silk. But the web doesn't break.

Spiders use their webs to catch prey. They also use their webs to communicate. They pluck the silk like a guitar. The strands vibrate.

A garden spider spins its silk in a zigzag pattern.

Spiders can make webs in different shapes. The Pennsylvania grass spider's web is shaped like a funnel.

Male spiders pluck the webs of female spiders. This vibrates the strands. The female senses the movement. The male plucks the strands in a certain way. This tells the female there is a mate on her web.

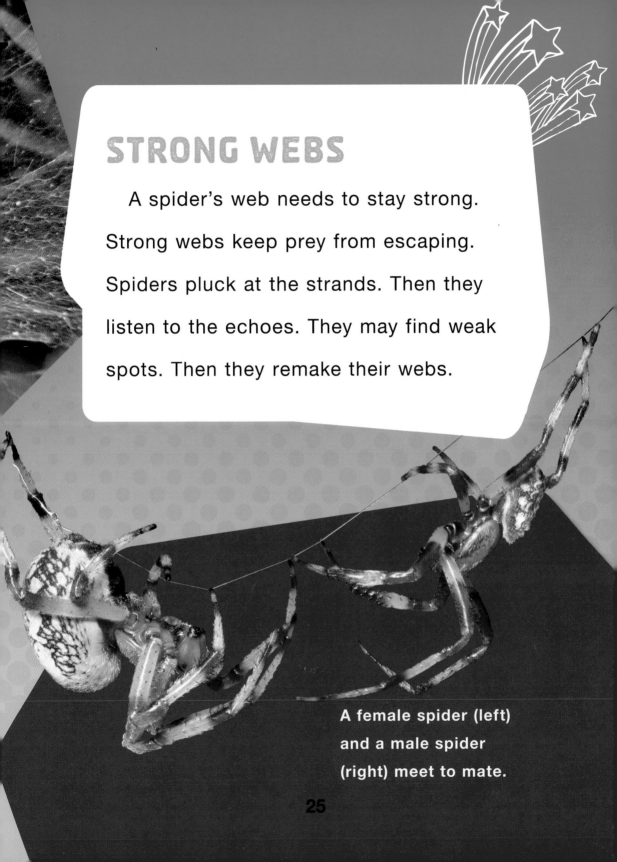

STRONG WEBS

A spider's web needs to stay strong. Strong webs keep prey from escaping. Spiders pluck at the strands. Then they listen to the echoes. They may find weak spots. Then they remake their webs.

A female spider (left) and a male spider (right) meet to mate.

PREY OR PREDATOR?

Some jumping spiders hunt other spiders. The jumping spider plucks the other spider's web. It plucks wildly. The other spider thinks prey is caught in its web. It goes toward the movement. The jumping spider catches and eats it! A spider's senses are powerful. But they don't always help it survive!

A jumping spider (left) hunts larger spiders by pretending to be prey.

SPIDER SILK

Some spider silk is stronger than steel.

GLOSSARY

abdomen
the back part of a spider's body

exoskeleton
a hard outer shell on animals such as insects and spiders

fang
a needle-like mouthpart that injects venom into prey

mate
a partner that an animal makes babies with

membrane
a thin layer of tissue that covers part of the body

organ
a part of an animal's body that has a special function

predator
an animal that hunts and eats other animals

prey
an animal that is hunted by other animals

sound wave
a wave formed when a sound is made

venom
a poison that is produced by an animal to defend itself and kill prey

vibrate
to move back and forth

TOP FIVE REASONS WHY
SPIDERS
ARE AWESOME

1. They use special organs and the hair on their legs to sense movements.

2. Their skeletons are on the outside of their bodies.

3. Their hearts pump blue blood.

4. Some spiders can catch bats in giant webs.

5. Some spiders spin webs while they are under water. They use these webs to breathe.

ACTIVITY

Spiders do not sense sound waves the same way humans do. Try out this experiment to discover how spiders sense sounds:

WHAT YOU'LL NEED
water

orange juice

vegetable oil

3 glasses

1 spoon

INSTRUCTIONS
1. Fill each glass with a different type of liquid. Put the same amount of liquid in each glass.

2. Hit each glass with the spoon. The liquid inside the glass will vibrate. This creates a sound. We hear these sound waves with our ears. But spiders would sense them with their legs and hairs.

3. Next, try using different amounts of liquid in each glass. Hit the glasses with the spoon. How does the amount and type of liquid affect the sound? How might this be similar to how spiders tell prey from predators?

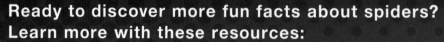

FURTHER RESOURCES

Ready to discover more fun facts about spiders? Learn more with these resources:

Barton, Bethany. *I'm Trying to Love Spiders.* New York: Viking, 2015.

Smithsonian Education: Under the Spell of Spiders
http://www.smithsonianeducation.org/educators/lesson_plans/under_spell_
    spiders/spiderspecifics.html

Want to learn more about different types of spiders? Check out these resources:

Guillain, Charlotte. *Super Spiders.* Chicago, Ill.: Raintree, 2013.

Marsh, Laura. *Spiders.* Washington, D.C.: National Geographic, 2011.

National Geographic: Black Widow
https://kids.nationalgeographic.com/animals/black-widow/#black-widow-
    sideways-web.jpg

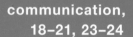

INDEX